ULTIMATE
PICTURE
PUZZLES

MORE THAN 200 VISUAL CHALLENGES!

THUNDER BAY
P·R·E·S·S
San Diego, California

Thunder Bay Press
An imprint of Printers Row Publishing Group
10350 Barnes Canyon Road, Suite 100, San Diego, CA 92121
www.thunderbaybooks.com

All correspondence (author inquiries, permissions) concerning the content of this book should be addressed to Thunder Bay Press, Editorial Department, at the above address.

Thunder Bay Press
Publisher: Peter Norton
Publishing Team: Lori Asbury, Ana Parker, Laura Vignale, Kathryn Chipinka
Editorial Team: JoAnn Padgett, Melinda Allman, Traci Douglas
Production Team: Jonathan Lopes, Rusty von Dyl, Susan Engbring

Cover design by Susan Engbring

Ultimate Picture Puzzles
ISBN: 978-1-62686-798-7

Printed in China
20 19 18 17 16   1 2 3 4 5

Contents

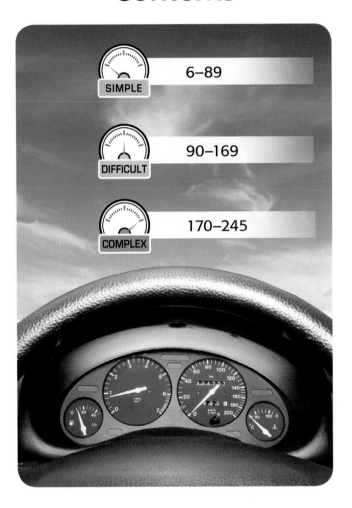

SPOT THE USAGE

Types of Puzzles

This book has three types of puzzles with one, two, or eight pictures on every page. Each puzzle may have five to ten differences, or an odd image that you have to spot.

ONE PICTURE PER PAGE

Compare the pictures on two opposite pages and spot the differences between them.

TWO PICTURES PER PAGE

Compare two pictures on the same page and spot the differences between them.

EIGHT PICTURES PER PAGE

Look at all eight pictures on the same page and spot the odd one out.

Symbols Used

1

Tick off one circle for every difference you find.

2

DID YOU KNOW?
Studies have proved that happy people live longer, make more money, and receive better job reviews.

The "Did You Know?" facts keep you interested as you go about spotting the differences!

3 | SOLUTION ON PAGE |

Help is close at hand. Just turn to the correct page to see the answers.

4

Record the time you take to find all the differences.

Difficulty meters

The sections are color coded to be in line with the difficulty meter. This is helpful in identifying the level of complexity of each puzzle. See how far you can push yourself!

SIMPLE

DIFFICULT

COMPLEX

Fairyland of sorts

Saint Basil's Cathedral, a Russian Orthodox house of worship, is located at the Red Square in Moscow.

DID YOU KNOW?
The structure of Saint Basil's Cathedral is inspired by flames reaching the sky. There is no such other structure in Russia.

SIMPLE

I TOOK

MIN : SEC

THE DIFFERENCES I SPOTTED

08 ○○○○○○○○○

SOLUTION ON PAGE 248

One step at a time

Established in 1872, Yellowstone National Park is America's first national park.

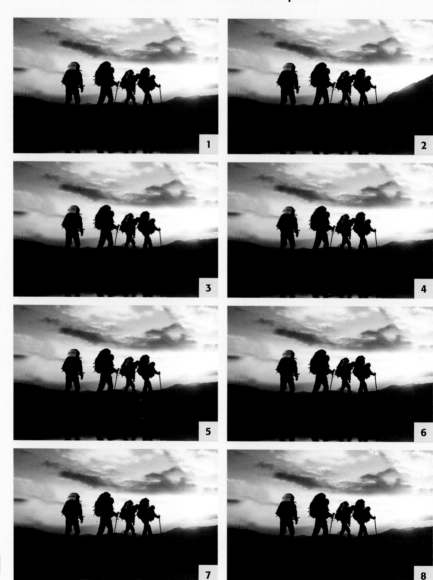

SIMPLE

I TOOK

MIN : SEC

SOLUTION ON PAGE 248

Cruising at our own pace

Can you find the odd image before these kayakers stop
to set up camp?

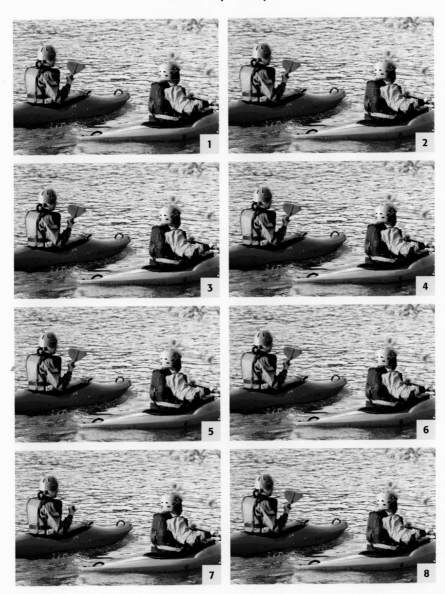

SIMPLE

I TOOK

MIN : SEC

Let us part ways

Find the differences between these two images.

SIMPLE

I TOOK

MIN : SEC

THE DIFFERENCES I SPOTTED

08 ○○○○○○○○

SOLUTION ON PAGE 248

Gliding along

You may not have eight arms to help you,
but solve this puzzle as quickly as you can.

SIMPLE

I TOOK

MIN : SEC

THE DIFFERENCES I SPOTTED

06

○○○○○○

SOLUTION ON PAGE 248

Traditional blue

In Morocco, one mustn't miss seeing the blue boats at Essueirra.

SIMPLE

I TOOK

MIN : SEC

THE DIFFERENCES I SPOTTED

06 ⟶ ○○○○○○

SOLUTION ON PAGE 248

Moscow: my winter land

As alike as these pictures might seem, there are seven differences.
Make the game even more fun by timing yourself while you find them.

SIMPLE

I TOOK

MIN : SEC

THE DIFFERENCES I SPOTTED

07 ○○○○○○○

SOLUTION ON PAGE 249

United in peace

"A smile is the beginning of peace."
— Anonymous

SIMPLE

I TOOK

MIN : SEC

THE DIFFERENCES I SPOTTED

SOLUTION ON PAGE 249

A boxer's handshake

American boxer Riddick Bowe is the only fighter to hold all four world title belts—IBF, WBA, WBC, and WBO.

SIMPLE

I TOOK

MIN : SEC

THE DIFFERENCES I SPOTTED

07 ⊕ ○○○○○○○

SOLUTION ON PAGE 249

Curled and cozy

Green Snake (1993) is a Hong Kong–based fantasy film adapted from the novel by Lillian Lee.

SIMPLE

I TOOK

MIN : SEC

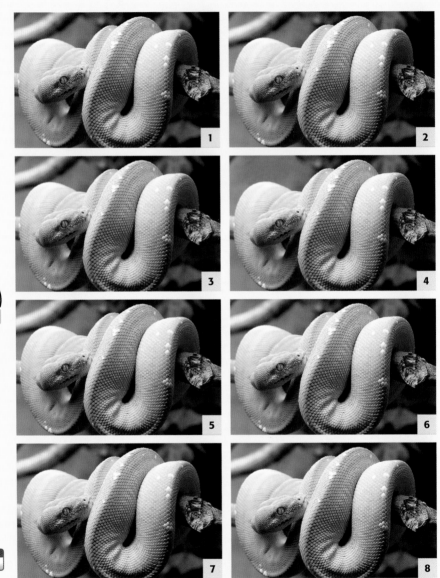

SOLUTION ON PAGE 249

Waiting for my princess

Tree frogs descend from the trees only during mating season, or under exceptional circumstances.

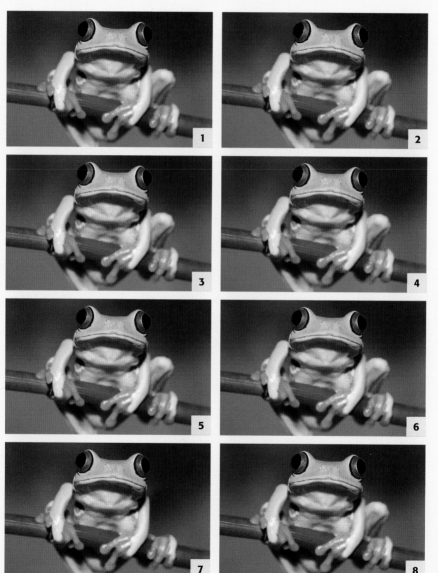

SIMPLE

I TOOK

MIN : SEC

SOLUTION ON PAGE 249

Away we go!

The city of London has breathtaking views. See if you can find all the differences between these two images of this spectacular scene.

SIMPLE

I TOOK

MIN : SEC

THE DIFFERENCES I SPOTTED

09 ○○○○○○○○○

SOLUTION ON PAGE 249

Greetings from Turkey!

The Topkapi Palace was the official residence of the Ottoman sultans for 400 years of their 624-year reign.

SIMPLE

I TOOK

MIN : SEC

THE DIFFERENCES I SPOTTED

07 ○○○○○○○

SOLUTION ON PAGE 250

Wheeeeeeeee!

The Native American term for snow sled is *toboggan*.

SIMPLE

I TOOK

MIN : SEC

THE DIFFERENCES I SPOTTED

06 ○○○○○○

SOLUTION ON PAGE 250

Something old, something new

"Whatever souls are made of, his and mine are the same."
— Emily Brontë

SIMPLE

I TOOK

MIN : SEC

THE DIFFERENCES I SPOTTED

09 ○○○○○○○○○

SOLUTION ON PAGE 250

Have you any wool?

The ratio of sheep to humans in New Zealand in 2005 was 12:1.

SIMPLE

I TOOK

MIN : SEC

THE DIFFERENCES I SPOTTED

06 ○○○○○○

SOLUTION ON PAGE 250

Follow me into the deep blue

Concentrate on the pristine and discover all the differences between the two images.

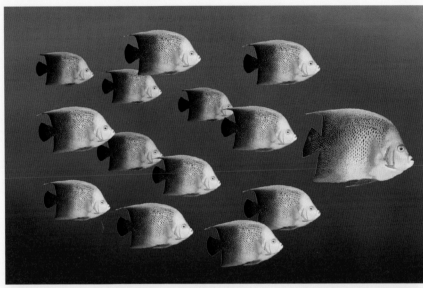

SIMPLE

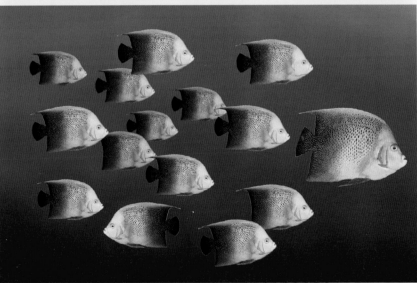

I TOOK

MIN : SEC

THE DIFFERENCES I SPOTTED

SOLUTION ON PAGE 250

Crimson light

All these lanterns may look alike, but there is one that stands out more than the rest. Can you spot it?

SIMPLE

I TOOK

MIN : SEC

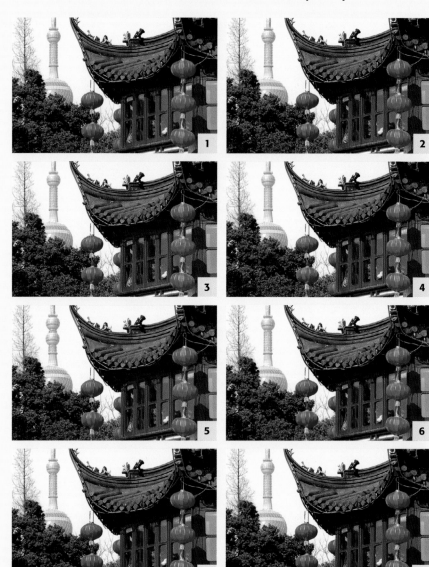

SOLUTION ON PAGE 250

Autumn evenings

"Autumn, the year's last loveliest smile."
— William Cullen Bryant

SIMPLE

I TOOK

MIN : SEC

SOLUTION ON PAGE 251

Winter wonderland

Even though these two images look alike,
there are eight differences. Can you spot them?

ULTIMATE PICTURE PUZZLES—SIMPLE

DID YOU KNOW?
Tom Sims modified the skateboard and made the first snowboard in 1963.

SIMPLE

I TOOK

MIN : SEC

THE DIFFERENCES I SPOTTED

08 ○○○○○○○○

SOLUTION ON PAGE 251

Odd one out

Due to deforestation, a majority of macaws are on the endangered species list. The Spix and Glauccous macaws are considered nearly extinct.

SIMPLE

I TOOK

MIN : SEC

THE DIFFERENCES I SPOTTED

07

SOLUTION ON PAGE 251

Being wise is hard work
Slowly and steadily, try and solve this puzzle.

SIMPLE

I TOOK

MIN : SEC

THE DIFFERENCES I SPOTTED

07 ○○○○○○○

SOLUTION ON PAGE 251

Grandeur for the best

The Boston Public Library (est. 1848) was the first public library that permitted people to borrow books.

SIMPLE

I TOOK

MIN : SEC

THE DIFFERENCES I SPOTTED

08 ○○○○○○○○

SOLUTION ON PAGE 251

Nothing like the warmth of home

Curl up on your favorite chair and relax while you solve this heartwarming puzzle.

SIMPLE

I TOOK

MIN : SEC

THE DIFFERENCES I SPOTTED

05 ○○○○○

SOLUTION ON PAGE 251

With you all the way

"Other things may change us, but we start and end with family."
— Anthony Brandt

SIMPLE

I TOOK

MIN : SEC

THE DIFFERENCES I SPOTTED

07 ○○○○○○○

SOLUTION ON PAGE 252

Male bonding at its best

"It is not flesh and blood but the heart, which makes us fathers and sons." – Johann Schiller

SIMPLE

I TOOK

MIN : SEC

THE DIFFERENCES I SPOTTED

08 ○○○○○○○○○

SOLUTION ON PAGE 252

Our favorite couple

As quickly as possible, try and spot all the differences between these images.

SIMPLE

I TOOK

MIN : SEC

THE DIFFERENCES I SPOTTED

07 ○○○○○○○

SOLUTION ON PAGE 252

We'll stare you down

Lemurs derive their name from the *lemure* of Roman mythology, which means "ghost" or "spirit."

SIMPLE

I TOOK

MIN : SEC

THE DIFFERENCES I SPOTTED

07 ○○○○○○○

SOLUTION ON PAGE 252

Bridge the gap

Find all the differences between these two images and solve the puzzle.

SIMPLE

I TOOK

MIN : SEC

THE DIFFERENCES I SPOTTED

07 ⬦ ○○○○○○○

SOLUTION ON PAGE 252

Because you can never have too many

At the Longhua Temple in Shanghai there are hundreds of golden Buddha statues.

SIMPLE

I TOOK

MIN : SEC

THE DIFFERENCES I SPOTTED

06 ○○○○○○

SOLUTION ON PAGE 252

Well done!

Try and find all the differences between the two images.

SIMPLE

I TOOK

MIN : SEC

THE DIFFERENCES I SPOTTED

07 ○○○○○○○

SOLUTION ON PAGE 253

Human pentagon in the heavens

Before this daring bunch opens their parachutes, try and find all the differences between the two images.

SIMPLE

I TOOK

MIN : SEC

THE DIFFERENCES I SPOTTED

07 ○○○○○○○

SOLUTION ON PAGE 253

A pair that helps

The donkey belongs to the Equidae, or horse family.
A male donkey is called a jack and the female a jenny.

SIMPLE

I TOOK

MIN : SEC

THE DIFFERENCES I SPOTTED

08 ○○○○○○○○

SOLUTION ON PAGE 253

The perfect day

Before the cows are finished grazing, try and spot all the differences between these two images.

SIMPLE

I TOOK

MIN : SEC

THE DIFFERENCES I SPOTTED

07 ○○○○○○○

SOLUTION ON PAGE 253

Do you have the time?

Marshall Field and Company, established in the late 1800s, was one of the biggest chains of department stores in the United States.

SIMPLE

I TOOK

MIN : SEC

SOLUTION ON PAGE 253

Ahoy!

The Boston Tea Party, which occurred on December 16, 1773, was a monumental event in U.S. history.

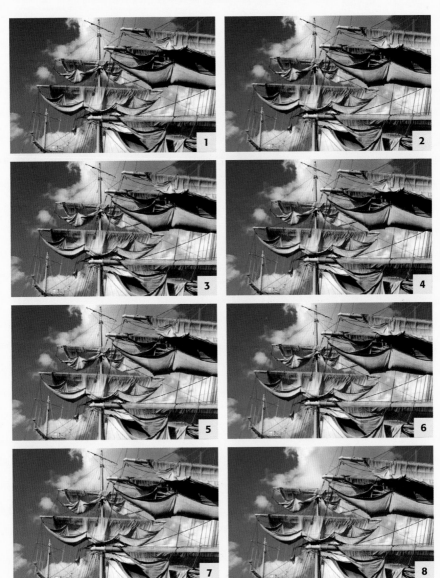

SIMPLE

I TOOK

MIN : SEC

SOLUTION ON PAGE 253

Step by step

Not a step out of line, but there are some differences between the two images. Can you find them?

DID YOU KNOW?
The process of controlling the climbing rope, which is attached to the climber, is called belaying.

SIMPLE

I TOOK

MIN : SEC

THE DIFFERENCES I SPOTTED

 ○○○○○○

SOLUTION ON PAGE 254

Free Willy

Keiko is the name of the orca that plays the role of Willy in the film *Free Willy*.

SIMPLE

I TOOK

MIN : SEC

SOLUTION ON PAGE 254

I'm not always crabby!

The Sally Lightfoot crab, at birth, is almost completely black and gains color as it matures.

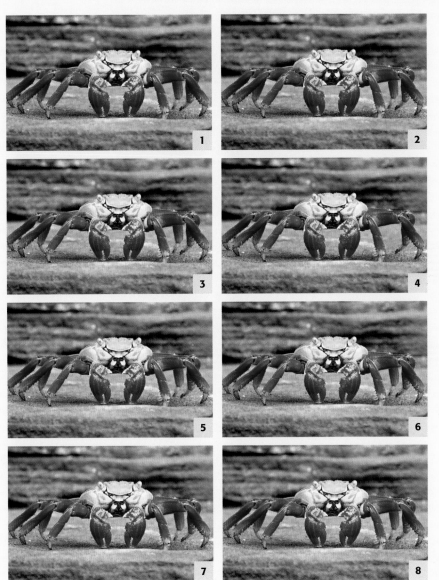

SIMPLE

I TOOK

MIN : SEC

SOLUTION ON PAGE 254

Holy city

Judaists believe that the Temple Mount in Jerusalem, also known as Mount Moriah, is the place where the divine presence rests.

SIMPLE

I TOOK

MIN : SEC

SOLUTION ON PAGE 254

The key of Hungary

The city of Szeged is the third-largest city in Hungary, and the University of Szeged is the second largest in the country.

SIMPLE

I TOOK

MIN : SEC

SOLUTION ON PAGE 254

Time for a sundown party!

Ibiza in Spain and Mykonos in Greece are islands that are popular for their crazy beach parties.

SIMPLE

I TOOK

MIN : SEC

THE DIFFERENCES I SPOTTED

06 ○○○○○○

SOLUTION ON PAGE 254

A trek to paradise

The High Tatras, a mountain range in Slovakia bordering Poland, is very famous for its treks.

SIMPLE

I TOOK

MIN : SEC

THE DIFFERENCES I SPOTTED

07 ◇ ○○○○○○○

SOLUTION ON PAGE 255

Thirst-quenching!

Sip on a refreshing drink as you try and solve this puzzle.

SIMPLE

I TOOK

MIN : SEC

THE DIFFERENCES I SPOTTED

07 ○○○○○○

SOLUTION ON PAGE 255

We love the sun as well!

Like these tortoises, you too could go outdoors and enjoy the sun as you solve this puzzle.

SIMPLE

I TOOK

MIN : SEC

THE DIFFERENCES I SPOTTED

08 ○○○○○○○○

SOLUTION ON PAGE 255

A trio of color

It is typical of trendy New York to keep reinventing itself in the simplest but most delightful manners.

SIMPLE

I TOOK

MIN : SEC

THE DIFFERENCES I SPOTTED

08 ○○○○○○○○

SOLUTION ON PAGE 255

Welcome to Madrid!

A statue of *El Oso y El Madrono*, which means *The Bear and the Strawberry Tree*, is the symbol of Madrid.

SIMPLE

I TOOK

MIN : SEC

THE DIFFERENCES I SPOTTED

07 ○○○○○○○

SOLUTION ON PAGE 255

Nothing like some good old sibling rivalry

Before the kids hit the water, see if you can find all the
differences between the two images.

SIMPLE

I TOOK

MIN : SEC

THE DIFFERENCES I SPOTTED

06 ○○○○○○

SOLUTION ON PAGE 255

Volleyed out

Beach volleyball was introduced as an official Olympic sport in 1996.

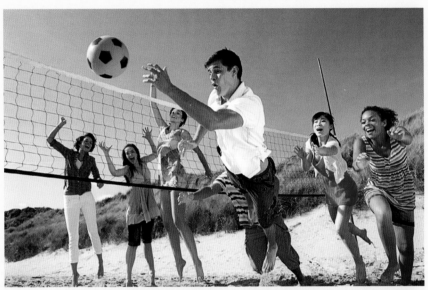

SIMPLE

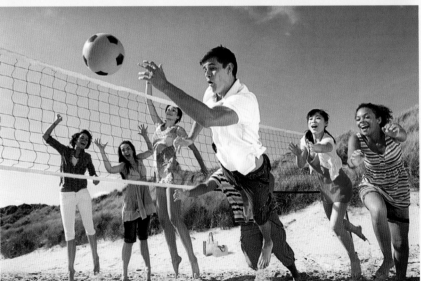

I TOOK

MIN : SEC

THE DIFFERENCES I SPOTTED

SOLUTION ON PAGE 256

Pink is the new black

In tenth century BC, flamingo tongue was considered an excellent delicacy by Romans.

SIMPLE

I TOOK

MIN : SEC

THE DIFFERENCES I SPOTTED

09 ○○○○○○○○○

SOLUTION ON PAGE 256

The furry pack

This pack is on the prowl for some fun.
Help them by solving the puzzle.

SIMPLE

I TOOK

MIN : SEC

THE DIFFERENCES I SPOTTED

08 ○○○○○○○○

SOLUTION ON PAGE 256

Where the wind blows

Amsterdam has eight windmills. The Sloten Windmill, built in 1847, is the only one that is accessible to the public.

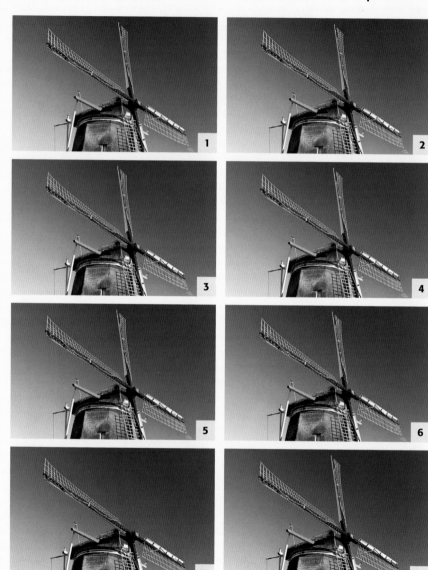

SIMPLE

I TOOK

MIN : SEC

SOLUTION ON PAGE 256

To keep life interesting

All these images may seem the same, but there is one that stands out more than the rest. Can you spot it?

1

2

3

4

SIMPLE

5

6

I TOOK

7

8

MIN : SEC

SOLUTION ON PAGE 256

Love, the ingredient needed for that perfect meal

"There is only one happiness in life—to love and to be loved."
— George Sand

SIMPLE

I TOOK

MIN : SEC

THE DIFFERENCES I SPOTTED

07 ◯◯◯◯◯◯◯

SOLUTION ON PAGE 256

The hills are alive with the sound of music

The alphorn, traditionally used by herdsmen in the 1800s, is the national musical instrument of Switzerland.

SIMPLE

I TOOK

MIN : SEC

THE DIFFERENCES I SPOTTED

08 ○○○○○○○○○

SOLUTION ON PAGE 257

Sharing is caring

Before the squirrel changes his mind, try and find
the odd one out.

SIMPLE

I TOOK

MIN : SEC

SOLUTION ON PAGE 257

Snack time

Can't decide which is more beautiful? That's okay, because to solve this puzzle you only have to spot the odd image.

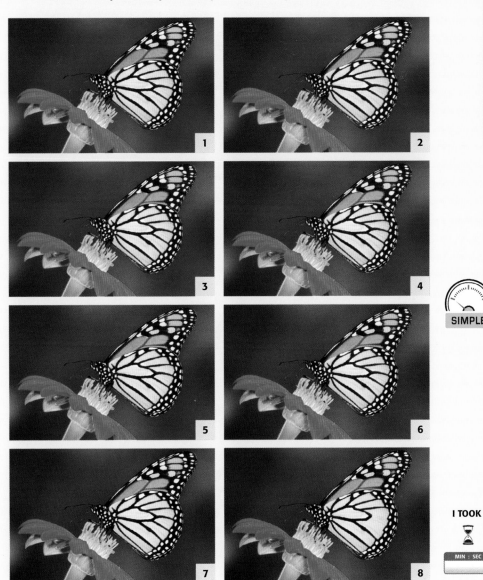

SIMPLE

I TOOK

MIN : SEC

SOLUTION ON PAGE 257

An apple a day

"Patience is bitter, but its fruit is sweet."
— Jean Jacques Rousseau

DID YOU KNOW?
Blackberries, concord grapes, and cranberries are the only native fruits of North America.

SIMPLE

I TOOK

MIN : SEC

THE DIFFERENCES I SPOTTED

08 ○○○○○○○○

SOLUTION ON PAGE 257

Sticky statistics

Systematically or otherwise, try and find all the differences between the two images.

SIMPLE

I TOOK

MIN : SEC

THE DIFFERENCES I SPOTTED

07 ○○○○○○○

SOLUTION ON PAGE 257

It's always fun with mom

While the little boy entertains his mom and little sister, try and spot all the differences between the two images.

SIMPLE

I TOOK

MIN : SEC

THE DIFFERENCES I SPOTTED

06 ○○○○○○

SOLUTION ON PAGE 257

Three's company

In sixteenth century, people of England believed that the Cavalier King Charles Spaniel could cure stomach ailments, and the dogs were popularly known as "comforters."

SIMPLE

I TOOK

MIN : SEC

THE DIFFERENCES I SPOTTED

06 ⦂ ○○○○○○

SOLUTION ON PAGE 258

Running like the wind

In Greek mythology, it is believed that the white-winged horse was the son of Medusa and Poseidon, and that Poseidon was the creator of horses.

SIMPLE

I TOOK

MIN : SEC

THE DIFFERENCES I SPOTTED

 ○○○○○○

SOLUTION ON PAGE 258

Dreamy city: Kolkata

Try and spot all the differences between these two images.

SIMPLE

I TOOK

MIN : SEC

THE DIFFERENCES I SPOTTED

08 ○○○○○○○○

SOLUTION ON PAGE 258

Engineering for the future

Amsterdam is famous for many a thing, architecture being one of them. Try and find all the differences between these two images.

SIMPLE

I TOOK

MIN : SEC

THE DIFFERENCES I SPOTTED

06 ○○○○○○

SOLUTION ON PAGE 258

A walk in the park

Solving this puzzle may not be as easy as a walk in the park, but it will surely be as fun.

SIMPLE

I TOOK

MIN : SEC

THE DIFFERENCES I SPOTTED

08 ○○○○○○○○

SOLUTION ON PAGE 258

For the fun of the game

"Some people think [soccer] is a matter of life and death.
I assure you, it's much more serious than that." — Bill Shankly

SIMPLE

I TOOK

MIN : SEC

THE DIFFERENCES I SPOTTED

09 ○○○○○○○○○

SOLUTION ON PAGE 258

The best ski resort

Just like these cute fellows, you too can have a jolly time.
Sit back, relax, and have a great time solving this puzzle.

DID YOU KNOW?

During breeding season, which occurs in October, there is a penguin safari in Snow Hill Island, Antarctica.

SIMPLE

I TOOK

MIN : SEC

THE DIFFERENCES I SPOTTED

07 ○○○○○○○

SOLUTION ON PAGE 259

A network in the desert

The Dubai Metro opened in 2009, making it the first
urban rail system in the Arabian Peninsula.

SIMPLE

I TOOK

MIN : SEC

THE DIFFERENCES I SPOTTED

08

SOLUTION ON PAGE 259

Horsing around

Thomas Ball designed the bronze George Washington statue in Boston's Public Garden in 1867.

SIMPLE

I TOOK

MIN : SEC

THE DIFFERENCES I SPOTTED

SOLUTION ON PAGE 259

Best friends forever

These women are enjoying a lovely evening. You can too while solving this fun puzzle!

SIMPLE

I TOOK

MIN : SEC

THE DIFFERENCES I SPOTTED

06 ○○○○○○

SOLUTION ON PAGE 259

Young love

In German, Valentine's Day is called *Valentinstag*.

SIMPLE

I TOOK

MIN : SEC

THE DIFFERENCES I SPOTTED

05 ⬡ ○○○○○

SOLUTION ON PAGE 259

Pretty in pink

Beat the clock! Try and spot all the differences between these two images as quickly as you can.

SIMPLE

I TOOK

MIN : SEC

THE DIFFERENCES I SPOTTED

07 ⬦ ○○○○○○○

SOLUTION ON PAGE 259

On vacation until Christmas
While on a break, solve this fun puzzle!

SIMPLE

I TOOK

MIN : SEC

THE DIFFERENCES I SPOTTED

06 ○○○○○○

SOLUTION ON PAGE 260

Too many cars

Try and find all the differences between these two images as quickly as possible.

DID YOU KNOW?
Beijing holds the top spot for being the most traffic-congested city in the world.

SIMPLE

I TOOK

MIN : SEC

THE DIFFERENCES I SPOTTED

 08

SOLUTION ON PAGE 260

Pink, yellow, or green?
Can you spot the odd image?

SIMPLE

I TOOK

MIN : SEC

SOLUTION ON PAGE 260

My precious bundle of mischief

Anna Jarvis founded Mother's Day on May 10, 1908, and President Woodrow Wilson made it a national holiday in 1914.

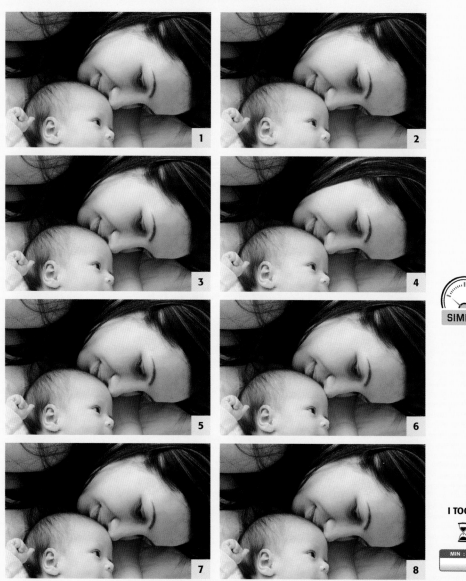

SIMPLE

I TOOK

MIN : SEC

SOLUTION ON PAGE 260

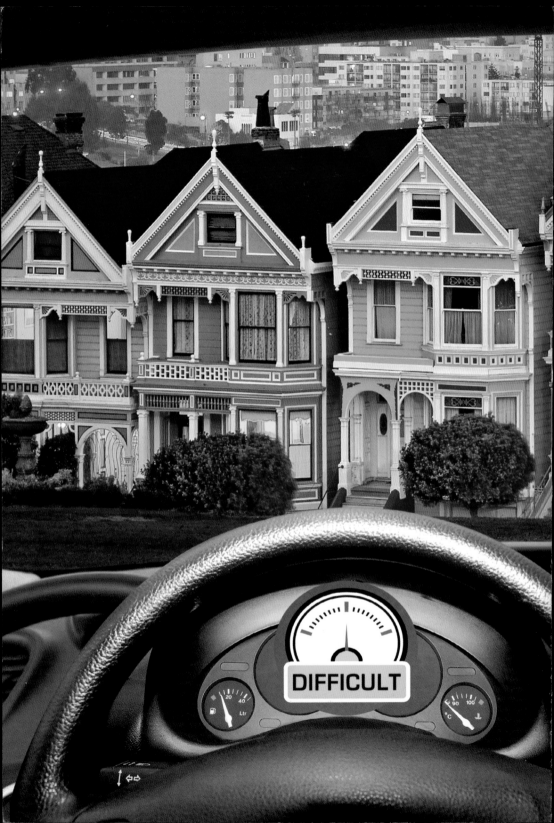

Triumph of will

These bison are determined to reach their destination. Are you as determined to find all the differences between these two images?

DID YOU KNOW?
Wild bison calves are lighter in color than mature bison. The rare white calf is considered sacred among Native Americans.

DIFFICULT

I TOOK

MIN : SEC

THE DIFFERENCES I SPOTTED

07 ○○○○○○○

SOLUTION ON PAGE 262

The Lion City

Singapore's original name was *Singapura*, which means lion.

DIFFICULT

I TOOK

MIN : SEC

SOLUTION ON PAGE 262

My ride, my city

"There may not be a heaven, but there is a San Francisco."
— Ashleigh Brilliant

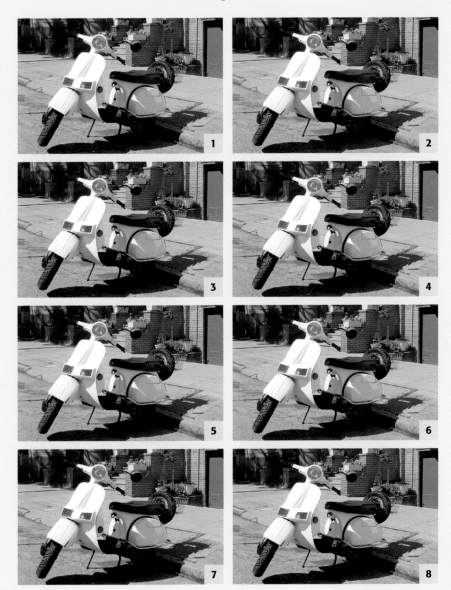

DIFFICULT

I TOOK

MIN : SEC

SOLUTION ON PAGE 262

There's nothing as nice as hugging mom

"If you have a mom, there is nowhere you are likely to go where a prayer has not already been." — Robert Brault

DIFFICULT

I TOOK

MIN : SEC

THE DIFFERENCES I SPOTTED

06 ○○○○○○

SOLUTION ON PAGE 262

Dinnertime

Solve this puzzle as quickly as you can.

DIFFICULT

I TOOK

MIN : SEC

THE DIFFERENCES I SPOTTED

08 ○○○○○○○○

SOLUTION ON PAGE 262

I will swim with you into the deepest blue

"At the touch of love, everyone becomes a poet." — Plato

DIFFICULT

I TOOK

MIN : SEC

THE DIFFERENCES I SPOTTED

06 ○○○○○○

SOLUTION ON PAGE 262

I have stripes to show off

Just as the caterpillar finds its way, see if you can find all the differences between the images.

DIFFICULT

I TOOK

MIN : SEC

THE DIFFERENCES I SPOTTED

08 ○○○○○○○○

SOLUTION ON PAGE 263

A garden of love

Central Park in New York City is one of the most romantic spots in the world and is very popular among locals and tourists alike.

DIFFICULT

I TOOK

MIN : SEC

THE DIFFERENCES I SPOTTED

08 ○○○○○○○○

SOLUTION ON PAGE 263

Changing of the guard

Before the guardsmen go off duty, try and spot all the differences between the two images.

DIFFICULT

I TOOK

MIN : SEC

THE DIFFERENCES I SPOTTED

07 ⟡ ○○○○○○○

SOLUTION ON PAGE 263

Deep blue sea

See how long you take to discover all the differences between these two pictures.

DIFFICULT

I TOOK

MIN : SEC

THE DIFFERENCES I SPOTTED

06 ○○○○○○

SOLUTION ON PAGE 263

Hai!

Dekimasu means "I can do it" in Japanese.

DIFFICULT

I TOOK

MIN : SEC

THE DIFFERENCES I SPOTTED

08 ⬦ ○○○○○○○○

SOLUTION ON PAGE 263

Lone wolf

The gray wolf is the largest wolf of the Canidae family. It is an apex predator, facing threats only from tigers and humans.

DIFFICULT

I TOOK

MIN : SEC

THE DIFFERENCES I SPOTTED

08 ⊙ ○○○○○○○○

SOLUTION ON PAGE 263

Natural elegance
"Calm, white calm, was born into a swan."
— Elizabeth Coatsworth

DIFFICULT

I TOOK

MIN : SEC

THE DIFFERENCES I SPOTTED

06 ○○○○○○

SOLUTION ON PAGE 264

Modern marvel

The Seattle Public Library's Central Library opened in 2004.

DIFFICULT

I TOOK

MIN : SEC

THE DIFFERENCES I SPOTTED

06 ○○○○○○

SOLUTION ON PAGE 264

Stolen heritage

In 1899 the 60-foot totem pole that had been taken from Fort Tongass by the Chamber of Commerce was unveiled at Pioneer Square in Seattle.

DIFFICULT

I TOOK

MIN : SEC

THE DIFFERENCES I SPOTTED

08 ○○○○○○○○○

SOLUTION ON PAGE 264

Skies of blue, fields of green
Can the child in you find the odd image?

DIFFICULT

I TOOK

MIN : SEC

SOLUTION ON PAGE 264

All smiles

Though the family looks perfect, there is one odd picture.
Can you find it?

DIFFICULT

I TOOK

MIN : SEC

SOLUTION ON PAGE 264

Cuteness lined up

Try and beat the clock by finding all the differences between these two images as quickly as possible.

DID YOU KNOW?
Hounds are classified into three types: sight hounds, scent hounds, and "others," which is any hound that doesn't fall into the other categories.

DIFFICULT

I TOOK

MIN : SEC

THE DIFFERENCES I SPOTTED
07 ⟡ ○○○○○○○

SOLUTION ON PAGE 264

In Los Angeles every day is a Sunday

"Don't grow up too quickly, lest you forget how much you love the beach." — Michelle Held

DIFFICULT

I TOOK

MIN : SEC

THE DIFFERENCES I SPOTTED

08 ○○○○○○○○

SOLUTION ON PAGE 265

Japanese autumn

"Autumn is a second spring when every leaf is a flower."
— Albert Camus

DIFFICULT

I TOOK

MIN : SEC

THE DIFFERENCES I SPOTTED

07 ○○○○○○○

SOLUTION ON PAGE 265

Magnificent wastelands

In Arabic the term "caravan" refers to the pilgrims and merchants who crossed the Sahara Desert.

DIFFICULT

I TOOK

MIN : SEC

THE DIFFERENCES I SPOTTED

07 ○○○○○○○

SOLUTION ON PAGE 265

Medical marvels

Can you find all the differences between the two images?

DIFFICULT

I TOOK

MIN : SEC

THE DIFFERENCES I SPOTTED

06 ○○○○○○

SOLUTION ON PAGE 265

Friends always make everything pleasant

"A good friend remembers what we were and sees what we can be." — Unknown

DIFFICULT

I TOOK

MIN : SEC

THE DIFFERENCES I SPOTTED

08 ○○○○○○○○

SOLUTION ON PAGE 265

Sweater, anyone?

Try and spot all the differences between these two images.

DIFFICULT

I TOOK

MIN : SEC

THE DIFFERENCES I SPOTTED

06 ○○○○○○

SOLUTION ON PAGE 265

Enchantment Avenue

As quaintly alike as these streets may look, there are eight differences. See if you can spot all of them.

DIFFICULT

I TOOK

MIN : SEC

THE DIFFERENCES I SPOTTED

08 ⟳ ○○○○○○○○

SOLUTION ON PAGE 266

St. Patty's Day!

Since 1962, Chicago has dyed its river green as part of the city's St. Patrick Day celebrations.

DIFFICULT

I TOOK

MIN : SEC

THE DIFFERENCES I SPOTTED

09 ○○○○○○○○○

SOLUTION ON PAGE 266

Happy divers

The word "snorkel" originates from the German word *schnorchel*, which was a tube used by German marines in World War II.

DIFFICULT

I TOOK

MIN : SEC

THE DIFFERENCES I SPOTTED

08 ○○○○○○○○○

SOLUTION ON PAGE 266

To the heavens and beyond

Try and find all the differences between the two images.

DIFFICULT

I TOOK

MIN : SEC

THE DIFFERENCES I SPOTTED

 05 ○○○○○

SOLUTION ON PAGE 266

It's that way. No, it's this way.

This couple, like most couples, is fuzzy about directions. As they figure out their way, can you figure which image is the odd one?

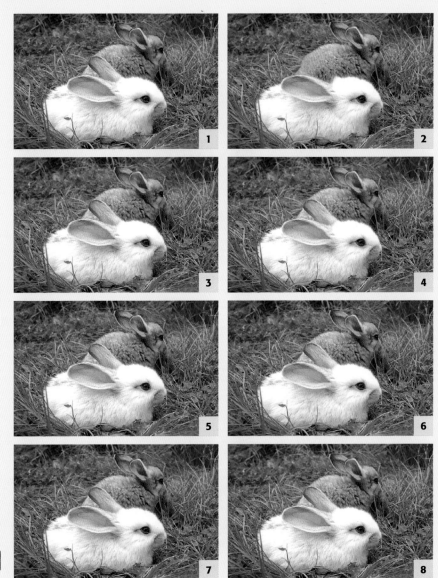

DIFFICULT

I TOOK

MIN : SEC

SOLUTION ON PAGE 266

Mom always knows exactly what to do

"Of all the rights of a woman, the greatest is to be a mother."
— Lin Yutang

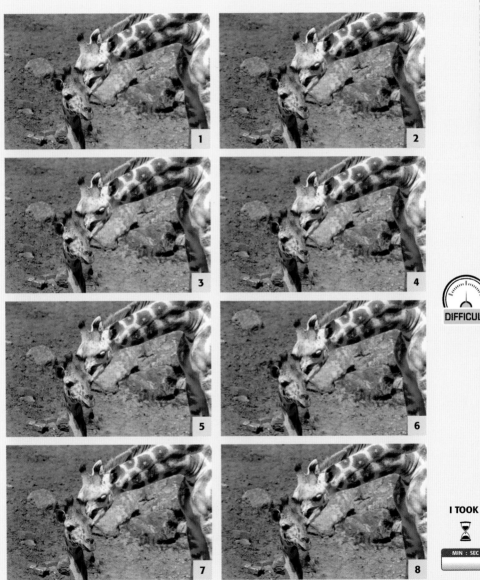

DIFFICULT

I TOOK

MIN : SEC

SOLUTION ON PAGE 266

Lined up
Try and beat the clock as you solve this pretty puzzle.

DID YOU KNOW?
Alamo Square is a residential area in San Francisco, California, characterized by Victorian architecture.

DIFFICULT

I TOOK

MIN : SEC

THE DIFFERENCES I SPOTTED

SOLUTION ON PAGE 267

Hey, all!

Try and find all the differences between the two images.

DIFFICULT

I TOOK

MIN : SEC

THE DIFFERENCES I SPOTTED

06 ○○○○○○

SOLUTION ON PAGE 267

Play me a tune

Historically, it is believed that the flute originated in France about 30,000 years ago.

DIFFICULT

I TOOK

MIN : SEC

THE DIFFERENCES I SPOTTED

 ○○○○○○○○

SOLUTION ON PAGE 267

A cheerful pair

Before this pair decides to fly off, solve this puzzle.

DID YOU KNOW?
There are about 370 species of parrots in the world.

DIFFICULT

I TOOK

MIN : SEC

THE DIFFERENCES I SPOTTED

08 ○○○○○○○○○

SOLUTION ON PAGE 267

Corridor to a better future

Rice University, one of America's best research schools,
is in Houston, Texas.

DIFFICULT

I TOOK

MIN : SEC

SOLUTION ON PAGE 267

Think about it

"If you can't dazzle them with brilliance, baffle them with bull."
— W. C. Fields

DIFFICULT

I TOOK

MIN : SEC

SOLUTION ON PAGE 267

Goal!

They're ecstatic that their team just scored. See how well you do at spotting the differences between these two images.

DID YOU KNOW?
*The first televised international soccer match was
between England and Scotland in 1938.*

DIFFICULT

I TOOK

MIN : SEC

THE DIFFERENCES I SPOTTED

06 ○○○○○○

SOLUTION ON PAGE 268

Up in the air

"Whenever you observe an animal closely, you feel as if a human being sitting inside were making fun of you." — Elias Canetti

DIFFICULT

I TOOK

MIN : SEC

THE DIFFERENCES I SPOTTED

09 ○○○○○○○○○

SOLUTION ON PAGE 268

Go green!

The Madagascar day gecko is a subspecies of gecko.
It is found in rain forests and mainly dwells on trees.

DIFFICULT

I TOOK

MIN : SEC

THE DIFFERENCES I SPOTTED

07 ○○○○○○○

SOLUTION ON PAGE 268

Kuznetsky Most

Since the 18th century, Kuznetsky Most, a street in Moscow, has been very popular for fashion and expensive shopping.

DIFFICULT

I TOOK

MIN : SEC

THE DIFFERENCES I SPOTTED

08 ○○○○○○○○

SOLUTION ON PAGE 268

With the correct attitude, everything is possible

The Palm Trilogy are artificial islands being built in Dubai, increasing Dubai's shoreline by 320 miles.

DIFFICULT

I TOOK

MIN : SEC

THE DIFFERENCES I SPOTTED

07 ○○○○○○○

SOLUTION ON PAGE 268

Nowhere to go but up!

"The best climber in the world is the one who's having the most fun." — Alex Lowe

DIFFICULT

I TOOK

MIN : SEC

SOLUTION ON PAGE 268

Every player needs a strategy

Except for America, almost every country in the world calls soccer "football."

DIFFICULT

I TOOK

MIN : SEC

SOLUTION ON PAGE 269

I rule this roost

"What is more miraculous than an egg yolk turning into a chicken?" — S. Parkes Cadman

DIFFICULT

I TOOK

MIN : SEC

THE DIFFERENCES I SPOTTED

06 ○○○○○○

SOLUTION ON PAGE 269

Count my spots

In the 1961 animated movie *101 Dalmatians*, the name of the cat that saves the 99 puppies from Cruella de Vil is Sergeant Tibbs.

DIFFICULT

I TOOK

MIN : SEC

THE DIFFERENCES I SPOTTED

07 ○○○○○○○

SOLUTION ON PAGE 269

Thai royalty

The Grand Palace is a complex of buildings that has served as the official residence of Thai royalty since the 18th century.

DIFFICULT

I TOOK

MIN : SEC

THE DIFFERENCES I SPOTTED

06 ○○○○○○

SOLUTION ON PAGE 269

Freeway express

California's magnificent network of freeways is evidence of the region's love of the automobile.

DIFFICULT

I TOOK

MIN : SEC

THE DIFFERENCES I SPOTTED

08 ○○○○○○○○○

SOLUTION ON PAGE 269

Balancing act

In 1974 French highwalker Philippe Petit stunned the world by walking between the towers of the World Trade Center in New York City.

DIFFICULT

I TOOK

MIN : SEC

THE DIFFERENCES I SPOTTED

07 ○○○○○○○

SOLUTION ON PAGE 269

We are family

"Families are like fudge—mostly sweet with a few nuts."
– Unknown

DIFFICULT

I TOOK

MIN : SEC

THE DIFFERENCES I SPOTTED

07 ○○○○○○○○

SOLUTION ON PAGE 270

The English countryside

Try and finish this puzzle in time for high tea.

DID YOU KNOW?
High tea is also known as "meat tea," as cold meats and eggs are served along with cakes and sandwiches—and of course the tea!

DIFFICULT

I TOOK

MIN : SEC

THE DIFFERENCES I SPOTTED

08 ⬍ ○○○○○○○○

SOLUTION ON PAGE 270

Piety in the city

Try and beat the clock while you solve this puzzle.

DIFFICULT

I TOOK

MIN : SEC

SOLUTION ON PAGE 270

The Venice of the East

Zhouzhuang is a Chinese village that has a network of waterways similar to those of Venice.

DIFFICULT

I TOOK

MIN : SEC

SOLUTION ON PAGE 270

Clowning around

To trademark a clown face, the Clown and Character Registry paints the clown's face onto a goose egg and it is archived.

DIFFICULT

I TOOK

MIN : SEC

THE DIFFERENCES I SPOTTED

07 ○○○○○○○   **SOLUTION ON PAGE 270**

Family fun

Universally, Children's Day is celebrated on the 20th of November.

DIFFICULT

I TOOK

MIN : SEC

THE DIFFERENCES I SPOTTED

08 ○○○○○○○○

SOLUTION ON PAGE 270

A slithery couple

Try and spot all the differences between these two images.

DIFFICULT

I TOOK

MIN : SEC

THE DIFFERENCES I SPOTTED

07 ○○○○○○○

SOLUTION ON PAGE 271

Now that's a smooth take off!

Seagulls are social birds and hence live in colonies.

DIFFICULT

I TOOK

MIN : SEC

THE DIFFERENCES I SPOTTED

06 ○○○○○○

SOLUTION ON PAGE 271

Hub of the Middle East

The Haydarpasa Railway Station in Istanbul, Turkey,
is the busiest station in the Middle East.

DIFFICULT

I TOOK

MIN : SEC

THE DIFFERENCES I SPOTTED

09 ○○○○○○○○○

SOLUTION ON PAGE 271

Made with love

Of the five most famous mosques of Istanbul, Sultan Ahmet Mosque, also known as the Blue Mosque, is the most impressive.

DIFFICULT

I TOOK

MIN : SEC

THE DIFFERENCES I SPOTTED

 ○○○○○○○○

SOLUTION ON PAGE 271

We are family

Find all the differences between the two images.

DIFFICULT

I TOOK

MIN : SEC

THE DIFFERENCES I SPOTTED

08 ○○○○○○○○

SOLUTION ON PAGE 271

A ball of fun!

Even though the two images look alike, there are a few differences. Try and spot all of them.

DIFFICULT

I TOOK

MIN : SEC

THE DIFFERENCES I SPOTTED

06 ○○○○○○

SOLUTION ON PAGE 271

Steady stroll

Before the turtle reaches its destination, try and find
all the differences between the images.

DIFFICULT

I TOOK

MIN : SEC

THE DIFFERENCES I SPOTTED

07 ○○○○○○○

SOLUTION ON PAGE 272

Beach bums at heart

Lion cubs are born with spots on their body, like those of leopards, and with age these fade away.

DIFFICULT

I TOOK

MIN : SEC

THE DIFFERENCES I SPOTTED

08 ○○○○○○○○

SOLUTION ON PAGE 272

Humble dwellings

Try and spot all the differences between these two images.

DIFFICULT

I TOOK

MIN : SEC

THE DIFFERENCES I SPOTTED

07 ○○○○○○○

SOLUTION ON PAGE 272

The jewel of Greece

Athens is not only the capital of Greece but it is one of the oldest cities in the world. Its history goes back more than 3,500 years.

DIFFICULT

I TOOK

MIN : SEC

THE DIFFERENCES I SPOTTED

06 ○○○○○○

SOLUTION ON PAGE 272

Nothing like your grannies to pamper you

"Nonna" means "grandmother" in Italian.

DIFFICULT

I TOOK

MIN : SEC

SOLUTION ON PAGE 272

Famous Five

The first of *The Famous Five* series, written by world-renowned author of children's books Enid Blyton, was published in 1942.

DIFFICULT

I TOOK

MIN : SEC

SOLUTION ON PAGE 272

Flames of the Caribbean

Try and solve this colorful puzzle as quickly as possible.

DIFFICULT

I TOOK

MIN : SEC

THE DIFFERENCES I SPOTTED

07 ○○○○○○○

SOLUTION ON PAGE 273

A sea of sheep

The first sheep to be brought to New Zealand was by Captain James Cook in 1773.

DIFFICULT

I TOOK

MIN : SEC

THE DIFFERENCES I SPOTTED

08 ○○○○○○○○

SOLUTION ON PAGE 273

The most crooked

It might be a bit difficult at first, but don't give up finding all the differences between these two images.

DID YOU KNOW?

*Lombard Street, the most crooked street in the world,
is featured in Alfred Hitchcock's* Vertigo *(1958).*

DIFFICULT

I TOOK

MIN : SEC

THE DIFFERENCES I SPOTTED

07 ○○○○○○○

SOLUTION ON PAGE 273

Lost bunny

One of these bunnies is lost. Can you find him?

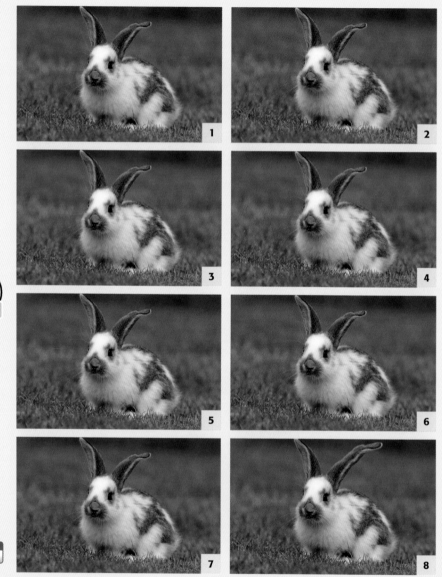

DIFFICULT

I TOOK

MIN : SEC

SOLUTION ON PAGE 273

Do not disturb!

The shell of a box turtle has a hinge at the bottom, so that it can seal itself up and escape from predators.

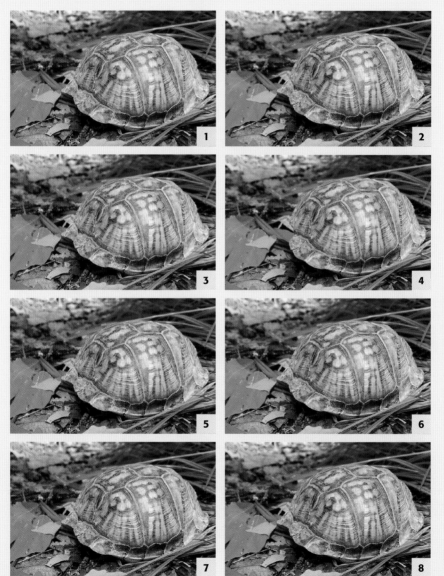

DIFFICULT

I TOOK

MIN : SEC

SOLUTION ON PAGE 273

Cheers!

Before they order the next round, can you spot all the differences between these two images?

DID YOU KNOW?

In the 1790s, "happy hour" began at three o'clock in the afternoon and cocktails continued until dinner, at which only wine would be served.

COMPLEX

I TOOK

MIN : SEC

THE DIFFERENCES I SPOTTED

09 ○○○○○○○○○

SOLUTION ON PAGE 276

Madame butterfly

According to *Kwaidan: Stories and Studies of Strange Things* by Lafcadio Hearn, a butterfly symbolizes a person's soul in all its different stages.

COMPLEX

I TOOK

MIN : SEC

SOLUTION ON PAGE 276

Coiled and cozy

Try and find the difference before our slithery friend wakes up.

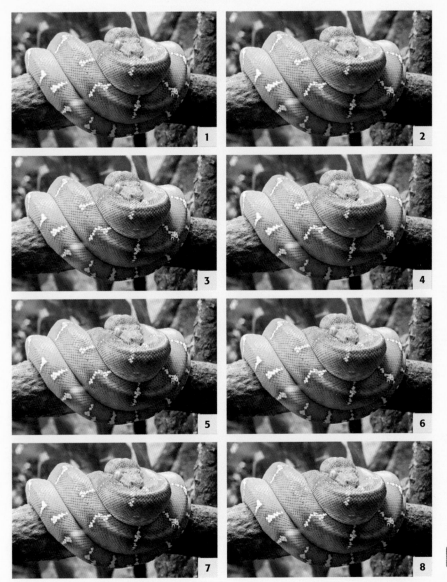

COMPLEX

I TOOK

MIN : SEC

SOLUTION ON PAGE 276

Behind the scenes

Try and beat the clock as you spot all the differences between these two images and solve the puzzle.

COMPLEX

I TOOK

MIN : SEC

THE DIFFERENCES I SPOTTED

07 ○○○○○○○

SOLUTION ON PAGE 276

Cairo from my window

Cairo is the capital of Egypt, and not only is it the largest city of the Arab world, it's also the largest in Africa.

COMPLEX

I TOOK

MIN : SEC

THE DIFFERENCES I SPOTTED

06 ○○○○○○

SOLUTION ON PAGE 276

Engineering for tomorrow

See if you can find a way to spot all the differences between these images.

COMPLEX

I TOOK

MIN : SEC

THE DIFFERENCES I SPOTTED

07 ○○○○○○○

SOLUTION ON PAGE 276

Make-or-break moments

Before the deal is closed, can you spot all the differences between the two images?

I TOOK

THE DIFFERENCES I SPOTTED

07 ○○○○○○○

SOLUTION ON PAGE 277

ULTIMATE PICTURE PUZZLES—COMPLEX

Moove over

Without getting lost in the English countryside, try and find all the differences between these images.

COMPLEX

I TOOK

MIN : SEC

THE DIFFERENCES I SPOTTED

07 ○○○○○○○

SOLUTION ON PAGE 277

Pretty in blue

"When you fish for love, bait with your heart, not your brain."
— Mark Twain

COMPLEX

I TOOK

MIN : SEC

THE DIFFERENCES I SPOTTED

07 ⟩ ○○○○○○○

SOLUTION ON PAGE 277

Reaching new heights of imagination

The earliest dated record of a settlement in Dubai goes back to 1799, and it was just known as an arid desert land. Today, due to its oil-driven economy, Dubai is a global business hub.

COMPLEX

I TOOK

MIN : SEC

THE DIFFERENCES I SPOTTED

07 ○○○○○○○

SOLUTION ON PAGE 277

Rush hour

Can you find all the differences in this busy rush-hour scene?

COMPLEX

I TOOK

MIN : SEC

THE DIFFERENCES I SPOTTED

 ○○○○○○

SOLUTION ON PAGE 277

If looks could kill

In the 1970s, Abraham and Strauss, a mega department store based in New York City, made mannequin modeling popular.

COMPLEX

I TOOK

MIN : SEC

SOLUTION ON PAGE 277

Mind over matter

All the mess is distracting, so they tried to clean up.
Can you spot the difference?

COMPLEX

I TOOK

MIN : SEC

SOLUTION ON PAGE 278

Just ducky

While these ducks enjoy their winter wonderland,
enjoy solving this mind-boggling puzzle!

DID YOU KNOW?
One of the species of duck that winters in Illinois, the Old Squaw is named so because of its noisy nature.

COMPLEX

I TOOK

MIN : SEC

THE DIFFERENCES I SPOTTED

SOLUTION ON PAGE 278

ULTIMATE PICTURE PUZZLES—COMPLEX

Calm canals

One of these canals is different from the rest. Can you spot it?

COMPLEX

I TOOK

MIN : SEC

SOLUTION ON PAGE 278

A landmark of time

Flora Fountain, built in 1864, is one of Mumbai's most distinctive structures. Atop the fountain is a depiction of the Roman goddess Flora.

COMPLEX

I TOOK

MIN : SEC

SOLUTION ON PAGE 278

Wonders never cease

Statins lower cholesterol, reducing the chances of
heart attacks and strokes.

COMPLEX

I TOOK

MIN : SEC

THE DIFFERENCES I SPOTTED

06 ○○○○○○

SOLUTION ON PAGE 278

Rock on!

As they pump out the beats, do you think you can find all the differences between the two images?

COMPLEX

I TOOK

MIN : SEC

THE DIFFERENCES I SPOTTED

08 ○○○○○○○○

SOLUTION ON PAGE 278

Flamingo lagoon

Chilean flamingoes have gray legs but distinctly pink knees and large black bills. Young chicks lack color and are mostly gray all over.

COMPLEX

I TOOK

MIN : SEC

THE DIFFERENCES I SPOTTED

09 ○○○○○○○○○

SOLUTION ON PAGE 279

Cool cat

Andrew Lloyd Webber's musical *Cats* is based on T. S. Eliot's *Old Possum's Book of Practical Cats*.

COMPLEX

I TOOK

MIN : SEC

THE DIFFERENCES I SPOTTED

08 ○○○○○○○○

SOLUTION ON PAGE 279

The technicolor life

Spot all the differences between these two images.

COMPLEX

I TOOK

MIN : SEC

THE DIFFERENCES I SPOTTED

07 ○○○○○○○

SOLUTION ON PAGE 279

Connecting people

"The road to success is always under construction."
— Lily Tomlin

COMPLEX

I TOOK

MIN : SEC

THE DIFFERENCES I SPOTTED

 ○○○○○○○

SOLUTION ON PAGE 279

Eat up!

As they enjoy this sushi, see if you can spot all the differences between these two images.

DID YOU KNOW?
Traditionally, the Japanese do not have sake with sushi as it is believed that since they are both rice-based, they do not complement one another.

COMPLEX

I TOOK

MIN : SEC

THE DIFFERENCES I SPOTTED

08 ○○○○○○○○

SOLUTION ON PAGE 279

A purrfect pair

The white tiger is not a subspecies of the tiger. The discoloration can occur in any species and is caused by a recessive gene.

COMPLEX

I TOOK

MIN : SEC

SOLUTION ON PAGE 279

The color in my life

The dusky leaf monkey is mainly found in Malaysia, southern Thailand, and Burma.

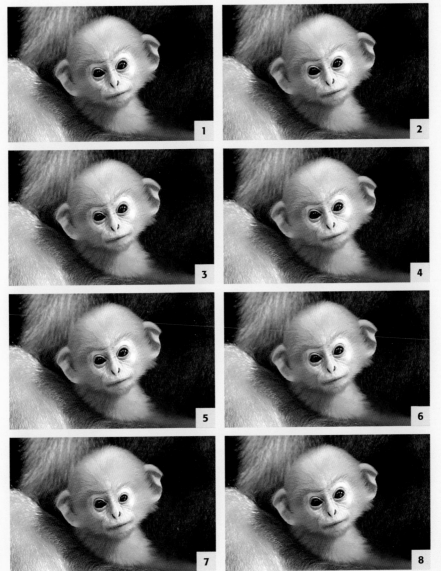

COMPLEX

I TOOK

MIN : SEC

SOLUTION ON PAGE 280

The shop of lights

Throw some light on the game by spotting all the differences and solving the puzzle.

COMPLEX

I TOOK

MIN : SEC

THE DIFFERENCES I SPOTTED

07 ○○○○○○○

SOLUTION ON PAGE 280

Let's go shopping!

Solve this puzzle as quickly as an impulse buy!

I TOOK

MIN : SEC

THE DIFFERENCES I SPOTTED

07 ○○○○○○○

SOLUTION ON PAGE 280

The hidden picture revealed

"Poverty is the worst form of violence."
— Mahatma Gandhi

COMPLEX

I TOOK

MIN : SEC

THE DIFFERENCES I SPOTTED

08 ○○○○○○○○

SOLUTION ON PAGE 280

A fortress of leaders

"In the business world, everyone is paid in two coins: cash and experience. Take the experience first; the cash will come later."
– Henry Ford

COMPLEX

I TOOK

MIN : SEC

THE DIFFERENCES I SPOTTED

07 ⬍ ○○○○○○○

SOLUTION ON PAGE 280

Burst of color down under

Coral colonies can live over 4,000 years. Dating back to the Bronze Age, the Leiopathes have been growing for 4,265 years.

COMPLEX

I TOOK

MIN : SEC

THE DIFFERENCES I SPOTTED

10 ○○○○○○○○○○

SOLUTION ON PAGE 280

Yes, deer!

All species of the male deer except for the Chinese water deer shed and then regrow their antlers annually.

COMPLEX

I TOOK

MIN : SEC

THE DIFFERENCES I SPOTTED

07 ○○○○○○○

SOLUTION ON PAGE 281

Amsterdam!

Amsterdam is the capital and the largest city in the Netherlands.

COMPLEX

I TOOK

MIN : SEC

THE DIFFERENCES I SPOTTED

07 ○○○○○○○

SOLUTION ON PAGE 281

Sky of hues

"Manhattan is a narrow island off the coast of New Jersey devoted to the pursuit of lunch." — Raymond Sokolov

COMPLEX

I TOOK

MIN : SEC

THE DIFFERENCES I SPOTTED

06 ○○○○○○

SOLUTION ON PAGE 281

The heat is on

The odd image is lost in the Kalahari Desert. Can you find it?

COMPLEX

I TOOK

MIN : SEC

SOLUTION ON PAGE 281

Say a little prayer for me

Can you spot the odd image?

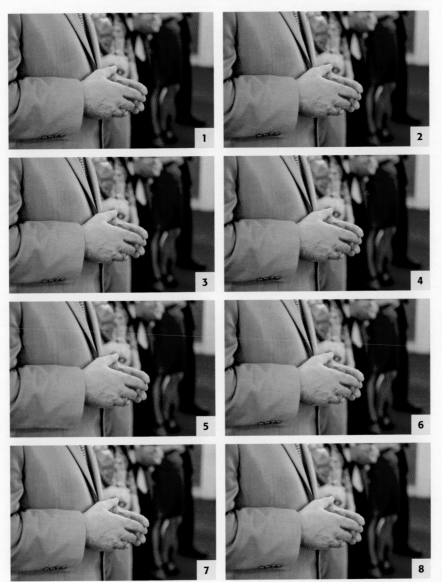

COMPLEX

I TOOK

MIN : SEC

SOLUTION ON PAGE 281

Full speed ahead

Wildebeest is actually Dutch for "wild beast." In Tanzania they are also known as *gnus*.

DID YOU KNOW?
When wildebeest cross rivers and other obstacles they do so as one; this is known as "swarm intelligence."

COMPLEX

I TOOK

MIN : SEC

THE DIFFERENCES I SPOTTED

10

SOLUTION ON PAGE 281

Stupefied

In AD 330, the Roman emperor Constantine moved the capital of the empire from Rome to Byzantium, now known as Istanbul.

COMPLEX

I TOOK

MIN : SEC

SOLUTION ON PAGE 282

Synonymous to Tokyo

"My heart that was rapt away by cherry blossoms—will it return to my body when they scatter?" — Unknown

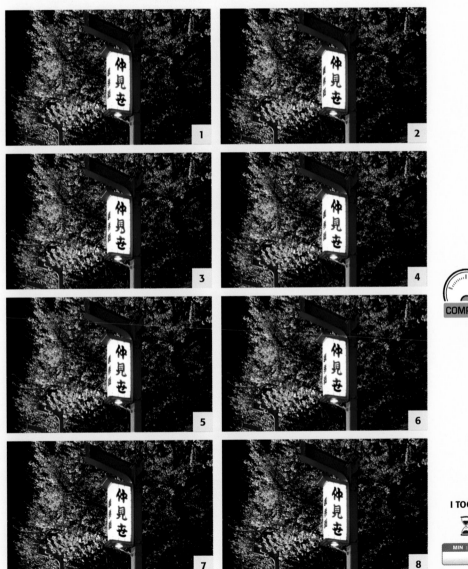

COMPLEX

I TOOK

MIN : SEC

SOLUTION ON PAGE 282

My station

The London Underground began in 1863, and, despite its name, more than half the network is above the ground.

COMPLEX

I TOOK

MIN : SEC

THE DIFFERENCES I SPOTTED

08 ⊕ ○○○○○○○○

SOLUTION ON PAGE 282

Luau mania

A *luau* is a Hawaiian feast where people eat, drink, dance, and make merry. Keeping that spirit in mind, enjoy solving this fun puzzle.

COMPLEX

I TOOK

MIN : SEC

THE DIFFERENCES I SPOTTED

SOLUTION ON PAGE 282

Time to come together

Until 10,000 years ago, lions were the most widespread mammals on the planet, second only to human beings.

COMPLEX

I TOOK

MIN : SEC

THE DIFFERENCES I SPOTTED

08 ○○○○○○○○○

SOLUTION ON PAGE 282

A chick chick here! A chick chick there!

Before Mama Hen takes her babies home, try and find all the differences between the images.

COMPLEX

I TOOK

MIN : SEC

THE DIFFERENCES I SPOTTED

06 ○○○○○○

SOLUTION ON PAGE 282

Majestic lights
The Palace of Catalan Music in Barcelona opened in 1908.

COMPLEX

I TOOK

MIN : SEC

THE DIFFERENCES I SPOTTED

07 ○○○○○○○

SOLUTION ON PAGE 283

Singapore skyline

Try and spot all the differences between these two images.

COMPLEX

I TOOK

MIN : SEC

THE DIFFERENCES I SPOTTED

07 ○○○○○○○

SOLUTION ON PAGE 283

I'm going to dance all night

Donna Summer, a performer from the 1970s, was one of the pioneers of disco and held the title "the queen of disco."

COMPLEX

I TOOK

MIN : SEC

THE DIFFERENCES I SPOTTED

08 ○○○○○○○○

SOLUTION ON PAGE 283

Serenading you

An orchestra has four kinds of stringed instruments:
cellos, double basses, violas, and violins.

COMPLEX

I TOOK

MIN : SEC

THE DIFFERENCES I SPOTTED

07 ○○○○○○○

SOLUTION ON PAGE 283

Walking tall

The Swahili name for giraffe is *twiga*.

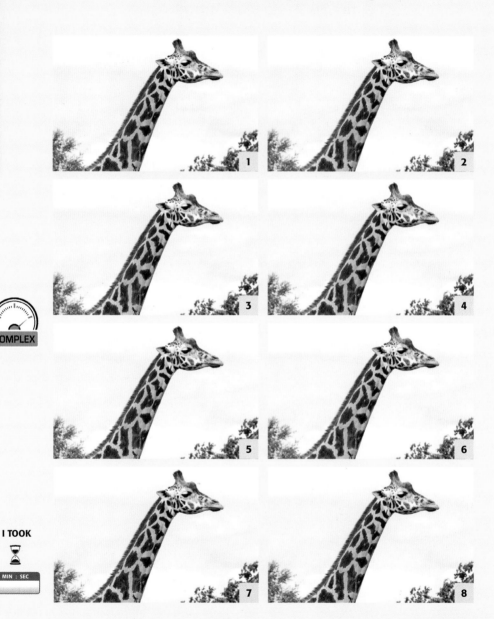

COMPLEX

I TOOK

MIN : SEC

SOLUTION ON PAGE 283

Let's not get nosy!

Baby seals are playful creatures and actually enjoy being tickled under their "arms."

COMPLEX

I TOOK

MIN : SEC

SOLUTION ON PAGE 283

Relief to my soul

"Flowers are Love's truest language." — Park Benjamin

COMPLEX

I TOOK

MIN : SEC

THE DIFFERENCES I SPOTTED

06 ○○○○○○

SOLUTION ON PAGE 284

City of the dead

There is a four-mile cemetery in Cairo. Many people live there in order to be near thier loved ones who have passed on.

COMPLEX

I TOOK

MIN : SEC

THE DIFFERENCES I SPOTTED

06 ○○○○○○

SOLUTION ON PAGE 284

Jet-setting genius

Before the flight arrives at its destination, try and locate all the differences between the two images.

COMPLEX

I TOOK

MIN : SEC

THE DIFFERENCES I SPOTTED

06 ○○○○○○

SOLUTION ON PAGE 284

One block at a time

Try and see if you can find all the differences between these two images.

COMPLEX

I TOOK

MIN : SEC

THE DIFFERENCES I SPOTTED

08 ○○○○○○○○

SOLUTION ON PAGE 284

No winter coat for me!

Spread over 20,000 farms, the Dutch sheep population is estimated to be 1.5 million.

COMPLEX

I TOOK

MIN : SEC

THE DIFFERENCES I SPOTTED

10 ○○○○○○○○○○

SOLUTION ON PAGE 284

A true romantic

"You don't marry someone you can live with, you marry the person you can't live without." — Unknown

COMPLEX

I TOOK

MIN : SEC

THE DIFFERENCES I SPOTTED

SOLUTION ON PAGE 284

Alaskan fishing

Alaska is famous for its Alaskan king crab fishing.

COMPLEX

I TOOK

MIN : SEC

THE DIFFERENCES I SPOTTED

SOLUTION ON PAGE 285

Now that's a view!

The Sydney Harbour Bridge carries both rail and vehicular traffic, and is locally known as "the Coast Hanger."

COMPLEX

I TOOK

MIN : SEC

THE DIFFERENCES I SPOTTED

 ○○○○○○

SOLUTION ON PAGE 285

A concert for inspiration

Try and beat the clock by spotting all the differences
between these images as quickly as you can.

COMPLEX

I TOOK

MIN : SEC

THE DIFFERENCES I SPOTTED

07 ○○○○○○○

SOLUTION ON PAGE 285

Flowery canopy

Add to the pleasure of solving this puzzle by stepping outdoors and enjoying the gifts of nature.

COMPLEX

I TOOK

MIN : SEC

THE DIFFERENCES I SPOTTED

08 ○○○○○○○○

SOLUTION ON PAGE 285

I'm no chicken!

Beat the clock and quickly spot the odd image.

COMPLEX

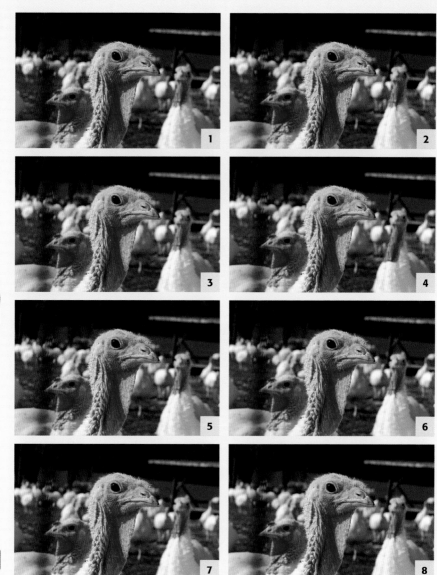

I TOOK

MIN : SEC

SOLUTION ON PAGE 285

Springtime

"If nothing ever changed there would be no butterflies."
— Unknown

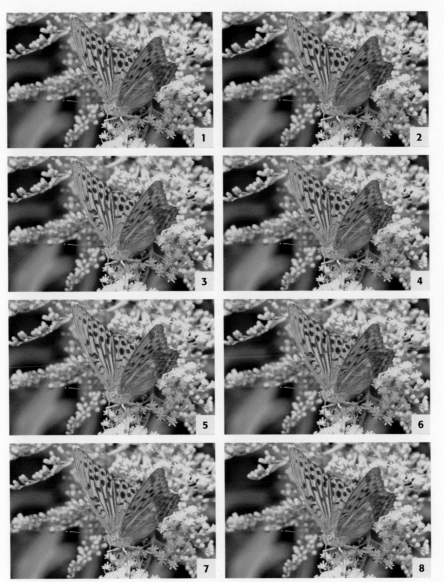

COMPLEX

I TOOK

MIN : SEC

SOLUTION ON PAGE 285

The glory of Moscow

Try and spot all the differences between these images.

COMPLEX

I TOOK

MIN : SEC

THE DIFFERENCES I SPOTTED

07 ○○○○○○○

SOLUTION ON PAGE 286

The Thai capital

Locate all the differences as quickly as possible and beat the clock while doing so.

COMPLEX

I TOOK

MIN : SEC

THE DIFFERENCES I SPOTTED

 05 ○○○○○

SOLUTION ON PAGE 286

Walking the holy path

Vesaka, informally known as Buddha's birthday, is an annual holiday celebrated by Buddhists all around the world.

COMPLEX

I TOOK

MIN : SEC

THE DIFFERENCES I SPOTTED

08

SOLUTION ON PAGE 286

Bring it on, let's race!

As quickly as you can, try and find all the differences between the images.

I TOOK

THE DIFFERENCES I SPOTTED

 ○○○○○○

SOLUTION ON PAGE 286

Our own waterfall!

Before the party ends, try and find all the differences between the two images.

COMPLEX

I TOOK

MIN : SEC

THE DIFFERENCES I SPOTTED

09 ○○○○○○○○○

SOLUTION ON PAGE 286

Chick-a-dee! Chick-a-doo!

The two images look alike. However, if you look carefully, you can spot the differences.

COMPLEX

I TOOK

MIN : SEC

THE DIFFERENCES I SPOTTED

08 ○○○○○○○○

SOLUTION ON PAGE 286

The secret behind flavor

The Mistress of Spices (2005), starring Aishwarya Rai and Dylan McDermott, is based on the novel by Chitra Banerjee Divakaruni.

COMPLEX

I TOOK

MIN : SEC

SOLUTION ON PAGE 287

High and mighty

Solve the puzzle by picking the odd one out.

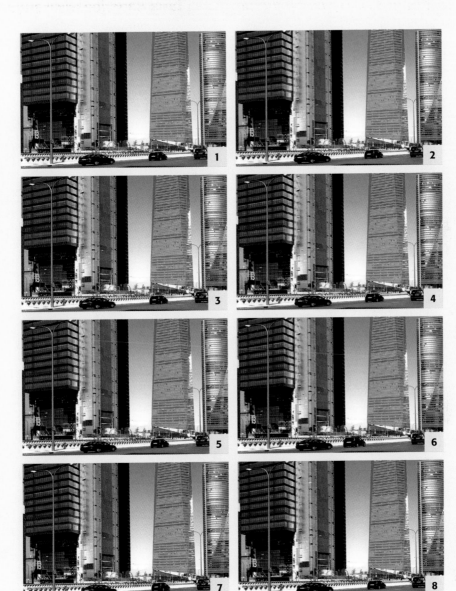

COMPLEX

I TOOK

MIN : SEC

SOLUTION ON PAGE 287

Rat race

"You don't have to be great to start, but you have to start to be great." – Zig Ziglar

COMPLEX

I TOOK

MIN : SEC

SOLUTION ON PAGE 287

Play the right note!

Before she stops playing, can you find the odd one out?

I TOOK

MIN : SEC

SOLUTION ON PAGE 287

Page 9

Page 10

Page 11

Page 12

Page 13

Page 14

Page 15

Page 16

Page 17

Page 18

Page 19

Page 20

Page 21

Page 22

Page 23

Page 24

Page 25

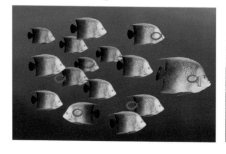

Page 26

Page 27

Page 29

Page 30

Page 31

Page 32

Page 33

Page 34

Page 35

Page 36

Page 37

Page 38

Page 39

Page 40

Page 41

Page 42

Page 43

Page 44

Page 45

Page 47

Page 48

Page 49

Page 50

Page 51

Page 52

Page 53

Page 54

Page 55

Page 56

Page 57

Page 58

Page 59

Page 60

Page 61

Page 62

Page 63

Page 64

Page 65

Page 66

Page 67

Page 69

Page 70

Page 71

Page 72

Page 73

Page 74

Page 75

Page 76

Page 77

Page 79

Page 80

Page 81

Page 82

Page 83

Page 84

Page 85

Page 87

Page 88

Page 89

Page 93

Page 94

Page 95

Page 96

Page 97

Page 98

Page 99

Page 100

Page 101

Page 102

Page 103

Page 104

Page 105

Page 106

Page 107

Page 108

Page 111

Page 109

Page 112

Page 113

Page 114

Page 115

Page 116

Page 117

Page 118

Page 119

Page 120

Page 121

Page 122

Page 123

Page 125

Page 126

Page 127

Page 129

Page 130

Page 131

ULTIMATE PICTURE PUZZLES—SOLUTIONS

Page 133

Page 134

Page 135

Page 136

Page 137

Page 138

6

Page 139

Page 140

Page 141

Page 142

Page 143

Page 144

Page 145

Page 147

Page 148

Page 149

Page 150

Page 151

Page 152

Page 153

Page 154

Page 155

Page 156

Page 157

Page 158

Page 159

Page 160

Page 161

Page 162

Page 163

Page 164

Page 165

Page 167

Page 168

Page 169

Page 173

Page 174

Page 175

Page 176

Page 177

Page 178

Page 179

Page 180

Page 181

Page 182

Page 183

Page 184

Page 185

Page 187

Page 188

Page 189

Page 190

Page 191

Page 192

Page 193

Page 194

Page 195

Page 197

Page 198

Page 199

Page 200

Page 201

Page 202

Page 203

Page 204

Page 205

Page 206

Page 207

Page 208

Page 211

Page 209

Page 212

Page 213

Page 214

Page 215

Page 216

Page 217

Page 218

Page 219

Page 220

Page 221

Page 222

Page 223

Page 224

Page 225

Page 226

Page 227

Page 228

Page 229

Page 230

Page 231

Page 232

Page 233

Page 234

Page 235

Page 236

Page 237

Page 238

Page 239

Page 240

Page 241

Page 242

Page 243

Pag 244

Page 245